Sonia

I really appreciate the friendship that we established throughout the years. You're support and kindness has put you in a class all by yourself. I hope my books brings the same type of joy to you, as knowing you has brought to me!

Thanks,
Melvin D. Katrie K.

SCHOOL BUS DRIVER
THE INSIDE STORY!

SCHOOL BUS DRIVER
THE INSIDE STORY!

Melvin D. Latnie Jr.

Mind Power Publishing • Ann Arbor, Michigan

Published by
Mind Power Publishing
P.O. Box 130086
Ann Arbor, Michigan 48113

Copyright © 1997 by Melvin D. Latnie Jr.

All rights reserved. No parts of this manuscript may be reproduced or transmitted in any form or by any means, electronic or mechanical, including photocopying, recording, or by any information storage and retrieval system, without the written permission of the publisher, except where permitted by law. Written, published, and printed in the United States.

Photographer and Illustrations Designer: Melvin D. Latnie Jr.
Editor: Lee Lewis
Illustrator: Mr. Roy Smith
Designed and typeset by Sans Serif, Inc., Saline, MI.

ISBN: 0-9648599-0-4

Dedication

I would like to dedicate this book to my late mother, Eula M. Watson. Although she is no longer with me, her memory still lives on. Her life and the way she lived it inspired me to start writing this book in 1990. Little did I know that she would be taken from me at such an early spring of her life on March 15, 1993 before the completion of this book. I hope that her continuance of life in me brings joy and knowledge to all that read this book.

Special thanks go out to: attorney Angela B. King, and Diane Khumayyis. Both outstanding ladies had praise and confidence in my writing ability when I myself did not. Your kind words and compliments gave me light in times of darkness. All praise goes to God for bringing your wisdom in me to surface at different periods of my life. One thought, one kind word, one action can make a difference. It did in me!

Kids, parents, and school bus drivers are the number 1 reason this book was written. When I think about all those doubters, and people with nothing but bad intentions who tried to stop the publication of this book, it leaves me with nothing but disdain for those who belittle someone's dream, and sorrow for those who give up. It is essential for kids to maintain a positive attitude in accomplishing their dreams and aspirations. Winston Churchill said it best: "Never give up, never give in."

Contents

Foreword ix

Introduction xi

I	How to Become a School Bus Driver	1
II	Tough Times, School Finances, and Triumph	5
III	Life in the Danger Zone	15
IV	The Caretakers	37
V	Kindergarten Posse	47
VI	The Good, Bad and Ugly	57
VII	No To Privatization	65
VIII	Special Education	75
IX	Baggy Pants!	79
X	Discipline	81
XI	The Unspeakable Crime	91
XII	The Last Day of School	95

Epilogue 99

Foreword

Melvin really shows the dramatic side of a job most people view as mundane. *School Bus Driver, The Inside Story* should be mandatory reading for any parent before placing their child on a school bus. School bus drivers everywhere will laugh, cry, and relate. Thanks, Melvin, for bringing us to light, and in such a positive light!

> Kathy Perry
> School bus driver
> Ann Arbor, Michigan

Kathy Perry

Introduction

It is amazing how many parents, day in and day out, send their kids to school every day without knowing a thing about the bus driver that transports them, or even takes the time to meet them. Although there are some substandard drivers, the vast majority of drivers are great. Most receive very little or no recognition for the super job that they do. The job, for the majority of school bus drivers, is part-time and seasonal. Yet it demands exceptional qualifications, a good driving record, and continuous training. One major problem in this fine occupation is the extremely high turnover rate. Countless new or inexperienced drivers are put on the road each and every year, putting our kids at risk.

On Wednesday October 25, 1995, in the small town of Fox River Grove, Illinois, seven high school kids were killed when a school bus driven by a substitute was struck by a train as it straddled the railroad tracks. The bus was driven by a supervisor not familiar with the route because the school district was short of drivers. I was in the final stages of writing my book when this horrible tragedy occurred. Then before the ink dried on my last entry, a Florida school bus was hijacked on November 2, 1995. Needless to say, the demands of driving a school bus are awesome!

This book was written by Melvin D. Latnie Jr., a former school bus driver who was promoted to the position of team leader. The book itself is true and well-documented, covering the school year periods from 1990 to 1997. It is an informative look at the

SCHOOL BUS DRIVER

good, bad, and humorous sides of public and private K–12 transportation, and life in and around the public schools. So buckle up your seat-belt, the ride is about to begin!

BUS DRIVER
Tolerance
Test

Now.... you do realize this is just a test. It doesn't come close to what THEY will put you through

1

How to Become a School Bus Driver

On August 22, 1990 at 2:45 p.m., I arrived for my interview. It was my first step in becoming a school bus driver. I had answered an ad in the local newspaper, and filled out an application and returned it to the Balas #1 Human Resource building. It was soon thereafter that I received an interview appointment with Kelvin Dobbins, transportation supervisor. He asked me a lot of questions pertaining to my employment history and work record. We hit it off well, and then he sent me to Diane Khumayyis, another supervisor, for a second interview.

Diane was very businesslike and asked very few questions. I got the impression that the decision to hire me had already been made. After the interview process was complete, Kelvin turned me over to team leader[1] Jo Anne Brown for an impromptu road test. The road test was very brief; it was basically just a gauge to measure how well someone could handle the large vehicle.

---

[1]Team leaders assist supervisors, the director, and drivers who need help with student conflicts. Team leaders also act as the liaison between parents, administrators, and principals. Their responsibilities cover everything from A to Z, including training new drivers.

SCHOOL BUS DRIVER

Jo Anne was very professional and complimented me on my driving abilities. I had driven large vehicles before in the military and civilian sectors, so the road test was not difficult for me. Jo Anne submitted a brief written observation to Diane. I then returned to Kelvin's office where he explained the training process to become a school bus driver.

When I was hired in 1990, a new commercial drivers license system was being established. By 1992 all truck and bus drivers had to convert to the new computerized system. Standards in the newly created system are very high because of past abuses, such as truck drivers going from state to state with bad driving records and several drivers licenses in their wallet. The new commercial drivers license is hooked up to a nationwide computer and only one drivers license is issued. Because of this, I was thrust into a new training program that was very detailed and thorough. Training was not paid until after acquiring sixty driving days on the job. Only after you completed your probation were you eligible to receive the paltry sum of $4.45 per hour for all the training time you accumulated.

Prior to starting the training program, I was informed that my pay would be $7.45 per hour; it would increase to $9.00 per hour after my probationary period ended. Along with my new hourly increase would come a whopping $50.00 deduction for union membership, along with monthly deductions for union dues. Mandatory fees were also taken out for the retirement plan. Starting pay for Ann Arbor public school bus drivers is now $10.39 per hour for the 1996–1997 school year, with yearly increases.

My newly assigned trainer was Jo Anne Brown, the same person who administered my basic skills road test. I can't say enough good things about Jo Anne. She did an excellent job in training me. Her attention to details, personality, and concern for the program were excellent. I went through the program in about five days, which was considered record-breaking for the new CDL course. I had to finish the program fast because I needed a paycheck in order to eat and pay my bills.

During your training you have to pass a written test at the Secretary of State office. I passed on my first try which is considered good, because most people flunk one or more sections the first time out. When I returned to work with the results, my road test was then scheduled for September 12, 1990. My road/skills test was administered by Maureen Meeks who is certified by the State of Michigan. The road test consisted of highway, city, rural and driving range testing. My final score was 98 out of 100 points possible. I could have gotten 100%, but that's another story. After I completed the road test, I had to attend and pass a mandatory two day safety course. The course culminated with a two hour test, pass or fail score. I passed with ease, because the commercial drivers training program was excellent in preparing me for both tests.

Note: Anyone contemplating becoming a school bus driver should seriously consider working through their initial training period unless they are financially secure.

SCHOOL BUS DRIVER

Balas #1, Human Resource Services.

II

Tough Times, School Finances, and Triumph

In January of 1996, I was in the final stages of publishing when our department experienced a change of leadership. By the first of February we would have a new director. It came as no surprise because of all the problems management and hourly employees were having with the former director. We now have a new director at the helm who has all the experience, leadership, qualifications, and personality needed to propel us into the next century. The majority of the experiences told in this book happened under the old regime.

On September 28, 1990, all new drivers were required to attend a CPR[1] course. The memo we all received said it was mandatory for our continued employment. "That's fine," I thought, "CPR is something that everybody needs." Soon disappointment set in when we learned that our time for the course would not be compensated. It had been a month, including training, without a paycheck. Times were so lean for me that when I opened up my practically empty refrig-

---

[1] CPR: cardiopulmonary resuscitation and emergency cardiac care provider.

erator, I could hear an echo from the sound waves bouncing off the walls when the half-empty ketchup bottle was inadvertently knocked over.

They said hard times make rational men do desperate things. I was about to do just that in the form of a letter written to the director on October 1, 1990. The letter basically reminded the director that only union drivers were compensated for their participation in the first aid/CPR course. It would be only fair and just if new drivers were compensated as well. Also, it would help establish a positive new employee/employer relationship, especially in light of the tremendous financial investment all the new drivers made in complying with the commercial driver requirements. I knew the letter could possibly put my new career in the doghouse, or worse yet, be used for termination later. But that didn't bother me—because my ketchup bottle was empty now!

Response to the letter was swift in the form of a written reply. In summary, the director said that because the new drivers had not obtained union status yet, there would be no compensation in any way for the mandatory class. My heart sank; I could feel the optimistic enthusiasm leave my body as my eyes scanned the curt letter. I knew none of the other new drivers had even attempted to obtain compensation because of the director's ominous presence and reputation. I was hoping for some minor financial relief for myself and the others during the probationary period, but it was not to be. The incoming tide of change would not reach the shores this time, but I held hope that the north winds would blow again. They did in February of 1996 when the new director, Diane Khumayyis, took the helm.

TOUGH TIMES, SCHOOL FINANCES, AND TRIUMPH

Mrs. Annette Taylor Janke, bus #39, June 1994.

All over the country public schools are being held more accountable for the tremendous amount of money that is allocated for each student. Some school districts across the nations have squandered money on superficial trappings in the name of education. Do they really care? Or has greed taken over the automatic state dollars received?

For example, when I think of Richmond, California, I'm haunted by the fact that the same thing could happen to districts all across the country. The story first appeared in the April 30, 1991, edition of Detroit's daily newspaper. It talked about how former superintendent

SCHOOL BUS DRIVER

*Dicken Elementary—bus 50, 1993–94 school year
Hang in there!*

Walter Marks bankrupted the school district. Marks spent money like it was going out of style. He indulged in excess on things such as expensive musical instruments, luxury furniture, extravagant furnishings, etc.

I cringe when I see all the instruments left on my bus and others that kids use free, compliments of the school district. I remember how my parents had to sacrifice and save just to get enough money to finance my instrument. Absolutely nothing was free. After he left the Richmond school district broke, Marks amazingly got a job as the new Kansas City school superintendent. The good old boy network took care of him.

TOUGH TIMES, SCHOOL FINANCES, AND TRIUMPH

All across the nation, public school finances are often talked about at school board meetings and family dinner tables. Where does that six to nine thousand dollars per student go? The bulk of it goes toward teacher salaries—although I exult in the fantastic job they do in this deteriorating American society.

Teachers' and administrators' salaries make up 75 to 80 percent of the total school budget in just about every district in the nation. In 1994 the average teacher in Ann Arbor made more than $50,000 for 180 days of teaching. Their powerful union and salaries prompted Governor Engler to bring about school finance reform. He passed legislation that increased the sales tax, and punished teachers with severe penalties for striking. I don't agree with the legislation passed by Governor Engler. It is hard to convince the teacher who has to deal with the lack of textbooks, teenage violence, drugs, and the problems associated with the breakup of the two-

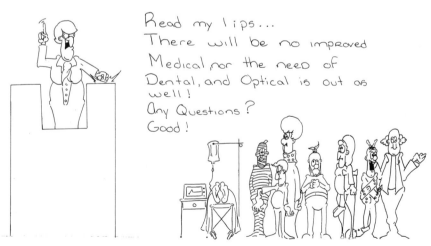

The Fight for respect never ends.

parent family that he or she is making too much money.

Despite the belt-tightening by districts all across the country, education is a multi-billion dollar business with colleges and public schools making millions of dollars in profits each year. Schools are the recipients of taxes, lottery revenue, and even corporate donations. The vast amount of revenue makes it hard for teachers to believe the money is not there. Take, for example, the Detroit public schools. They had a six million dollar surplus in 1990, and were expected to make four million dollars for the 1991 school year, as reported in the May 8, 1991 edition of the *Detroit Free Press*.

The lack of money is not the problem in the public schools; it is the way in which the money is spent. For example, Iowa ranks high in scholastic testing each year, spending a fraction of the revenue other states spend per student. Low crime and divorce rates contribute to their success. It is much easier for a child to learn when both parents are in the home and showing an interest in their education.

School finances are always important. Every parent wants their school to be on good financial ground, even if they are not. I will never forget the winter of 1994, when I was doing route 79. One of my stops was at the government-subsidized Arrowwood Housing Complex. The temperature on that December day was a little warmer than usual. All the kids had departed in the morning. I did my routine bus inspection and discovered a boy's coat with no recognizable name on the label. There was a name on the coat, but it was not the name of any of my riding students or students that attended Thurston Elementary.

TOUGH TIMES, SCHOOL FINANCES, AND TRIUMPH

When the kids boarded that afternoon, I held the coat up high and asked them if they knew who it belonged to. Then I read the name on the label. No one answered. The following morning I repeated the whole process. Again no one answered. Then all the students departed the bus but one. Kevin[2] purposely stayed behind. Kevin is about four and a half feet tall, a thin second-grader with light brown eyes and an amber complexion. He started walking up to me slowly with his head bowed, shoulders slumped, and tears running down his face. As he approached, I was thinking, "Why is he so sad?"

It must have seemed like an eternity to him walking from the rear of the bus to the front. When he finally arrived he said, "That's my coat."

"Are you sure? It has a different name on it, and you have a coat on."

"I'm sure. The coat I have on is my brother's, and that coat (pointing), my mother got it free from the Goodwill."

I immediately handed it to him and said, "Take care, my friend. I'll see you later." After he departed the bus, I could feel my eyes welling with emotion. The little guy didn't want anyone to know he got his coat secondhand from Goodwill.

So often we become so involved in our own daily struggles that we forget there's somebody else worse off than we are. The Ann Arbor school district contains a number of affluent neighborhoods, but still there are pockets of families struggling to make ends meet.

---

[2]The majority of the students' and parents' names have been changed to protect their privacy.

SCHOOL BUS DRIVER

Close your eyes and try to imagine that you're a single mother with four kids, struggling to put food on the table with $8,000 of government aid in the form of food stamps and rent stipends. Your kids attend a public school where it's not unusual for kindergartners to wear $150 Michael Jordan basketball shoes, and some high school students drive to school in their own convertible Mustang GT. You have a teenage son who is twice your size, and he wears his pants around his thighs showing underwear nobody wants to see. His father is in jail. And he only attends class when he can sport a new Fila outfit from his gambling proceeds. After countless hours of fruitless counseling, your pride and joy will be labeled vexatious and sent to the waiting arms of principal Joe Dulin.

Architectural design supreme, Ann Arbor Huron High.

TOUGH TIMES, SCHOOL FINANCES, AND TRIUMPH

The old and dilapidated Roberto Clemente School; May 1991.

The new Roberto Clemente School; July 1994.

SCHOOL BUS DRIVER

Roberto Clemente: "A+" for a job well done; June 8, 1996.

Now you can stop imagining. Joe Dulin heads the very successful Ann Arbor public schools Roberto Clemente Student Development Center. For over seventeen years, the school had been isolated and ignored financially by all of the former superintendents. Now, since 1994, a new school proudly sits on Textile Road in Ypsilanti. The new school is furnished with all the equipment, technology, and teachers to provide a conducive learning environment that will enable troubled students to excel in life.

Life in the Danger Zone

I had been driving kids to school for about three weeks when the call came over the radio. Bus 65, driven by Janice P., was involved in an accident with a fifteen-ton dump truck. The bus was filled with kids at the time, and all you could hear was screaming over Janice's attempt to report the accident. The dispatch supervisor was calm and dispatched police and emergency crew to the scene immediately. Luckily, no one was seriously hurt. Later it was discovered that the reason for the accident was something that could and should have been avoided.

Janice, according to her students and other drivers, was engaged in an argument with the dump truck driver. The ensuing argument was over his trying to get her to go around the construction site, while she refused to do so. She wanted him to "get the hell out of the way." Neither would budge on this matter. So the driver got in his truck, put it in reverse and rammed the school bus!

One can only imagine what was on his mind. His stupid behavior could have resulted in someone getting killed. Needless to say, Janice's judgment was also in error. There is no logical reason for any bus driver to endanger the lives of students. Management also felt the same way, because Janice soon departed with her stubborn personality in need of a new job.

Wednesday, April 4, 1991

I had just finished my Pattengill Elementary run and had to hurry over to Scarlett Middle School for my scheduled after-school activity route. As I drove down Scarlett Drive, the parade of Ann Arbor police cars was an ominous site to behold. My thoughts were, "Oh, no. I hope this is not a sign of things to come." It was, but I wouldn't learn what summoned the strong law enforcement response until the next day.

Just prior to my arriving at Scarlett, the police had broken up a fight, later reported in the *Ann Arbor News*. The fight between two 14-year-old boys produced a crowd of about 70 teenage students. The two students, one from Scarlett and the other from Ypsilanti High School, had an ongoing dispute over a girl. The two were prepared to "get it on" when a Scarlett teacher broke it up and escorted the Ann Arbor youth home. Investigators said when the boy got home, his mother suggested a fight be arranged between the two "to settle the matter." The two boys and a number of supporters from both sides gathered at another location. They began fighting, but thank God it was broken up by police.

It's incredible to think that one of the parents actually instigated and promoted the fight. In this day and age of kids settling disputes with guns, it was absolutely stupid for that parent to encourage that the dispute be settled with violence. That incident came within a whisker of becoming a riot between two crosstown schools. It also was the launching pad for my violent evening. When I arrived at approximately 4:10 p.m., the parking lot was still scattered with students. I felt very uneasy seeing the last police car leave. Obviously I knew something had happened earlier, but

SCHOOL BUS DRIVER

the thought of not knowing exactly what occurred left my mind racing with Stephen King horror scenarios.

Students boarded the bus as usual with bus pass in hand. Then I noticed a new student board that hadn't ridden before. It didn't strike me as alarming because there were at least three to four new students that rode, on average, per week. I had to let him ride, by policy, because he had a Scarlett bus pass. I was 25 minutes into my route when the fight broke out between a female Scarlett student and the male, whom I later learned was a Huron High School student. He had deceptively obtained a bus pass from a Scarlett student. When I looked up, I was shocked and appalled to see this new male student hitting a girl with bad intentions. I radioed base, pulled the bus over, and immediately broke up the fight.

Despite his efforts, the dispatcher was unable to contact anyone from Scarlett. The male student was still seething and yelling, "I am going to kill you when you get off the bus, you stinking b——!" He was very serious. And I was stuck with the task of trying to get the students home. I could see the intensity and rage in his face as the veins in his neck and forehead bulged as if they were a pumping station for steroids. I had him sit in the first seat to the right of me, so I could immediately stop the bus—and him—if he decided to resume his human punching bag display. He was mad, and I could see him contemplating "taking me out" and finishing his violent attack. He didn't, I think, because of how quickly he was neutralized the first time. Image is everything for most teenagers! I prayed silently that he would stay seated, because I knew in my heart that I would do everything in my power to protect the young girl from additional harm.

The situation was growing more tense by the moment. The dispatcher's shift was over and he was out of there. Another supervisor took over the helm, and I immediately requested that she call the police. Apparently she didn't feel it was necessary, and instead called the girl's mother and requested that she meet the bus. I tried hopelessly to relay the gravity of the situation to her, but to no avail. Making matters even worse was the fact that both of the students lived in the same apartment complex. My brain was running at warp factor nine trying to come up with a safe solution to this nerve-wracking problem. I decided to let the Mike Tyson want-to-be out first at a different location and circle the complex until the girl's mother arrived. It worked. The bruised and slightly battered student called Kimbra made it home without further incident. I still shudder, to this day, when I think about how close that young lady came to being seriously injured.

May 21, 1991

One of the nice things about being a school bus driver is that you're outside, not tied to a desk or computer terminal. Last April's bus rumble really seasoned me as a new driver. I was starting to feel great about route 78 and enjoying one of those rare beautiful Michigan spring days when the crossing guard came into my life.

It was at approximately 3:38 p.m. Pattengill Elementary had just let out, and I was approaching the corner of Packard Road and Jewett Avenue. The traffic light was red at the time. Suddenly I noticed the school crossing guard across the street fall flat on her back. At first I thought maybe she had slipped, but she then proceeded to fall over and over again. By this time, it was total pandemonium from the kids on my bus.

The light finally turned green. After driving across the street, I immediately pulled the bus over and advised dispatch of the situation. When I approached the school crossing guard, I was overwhelmed by the repugnant odor of alcohol. I tried to get her to remain seated, and I told her I would have an ambulance sent because of the serious falls she suffered. She responded by repeatedly saying, "Please don't call the ambulance!"

Finally another driver stopped, and he also deduced what was very apparent. She was drunk, so drunk that she couldn't do her job. So drunk that she could have killed herself, or worse yet, gotten some child killed. The name from her ID card still stays in my mind—"Marion L." Lloyd Wafer, team leader, was in the area and he arrived shortly. He also was astonished to see the approximately 65-year-old guard in such an intoxicated state in the middle of the afternoon. Just before continuing on my route she repeatedly, through her slurred speech, requested that we call her husband. We

LIFE IN THE DANGER ZONE

immediately complied. He arrived shortly and transported her home safely.

I got the impression throughout the whole ordeal that Marion could feel the "Sword of Damocles" hanging over her crossing guard duties. Shortly after the incident, Ann Arbor police officer Van Dam contacted me for further details. That was the last day I saw Marion L. I would assume that she is no longer employed as a school crossing guard. Later I received special recognition from the transportation department, and a heartfelt "thank you" from the Ann Arbor police department for a job well done.

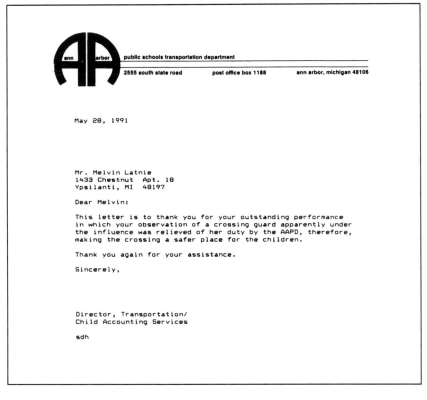

SCHOOL BUS DRIVER

*School bus 78 on a cold winter day at
Pattengill Elementary School, 1990–91 school year.*

I know my response to the crossing guard incident is a typical one for the vast number of school bus drivers. Our job is a tough one, but one that we take great pride in. When I was in the Marine Corps we had a saying amongst ourselves that went like this: "Not on my watch, nor my post!" I see that same pride exemplified in school bus drivers.

Looking back on my first year driving, there was no way I could have predicted the numerous events that shaped the 1990-1991 school year. It was a year replete with learning, joy, and heartache. I started the year with fervid enthusiasm, and by the grace of God, finished the same way. As the spring season died, the countdown to summer vacation blossomed. During

LIFE IN THE DANGER ZONE

Bzz... Stay calm maybe they won't see us Bzz...

Stay calm guys Bees won't harm you if you're calm

Come now, you aren't Remaining very calm

that period of the year, nature dispatches its army of bees to prey on school bus drivers without air conditioning.

I was traveling down Wisteria Drive with my Pattengill students when three yellow-jacket bees managed to board my bus through one of the open windows—causing total chaos. As the bees swarmed from the back of the bus to the front, kids were jumping on top of seats and running in every direction. Some were even hiding under the seats, doing what they could to avoid being stung. I pulled the bus over immediately and tried to bring order to the screaming and running kids.

Although the situation was serious, the looks on their faces were comical to say the least. I couldn't help but laugh inside as they appeared to imitate Michael Jackson while avoiding the hard-charging yellow-jackets on their search and destroy mission. I had to shout very loudly to get the kids to settle down. Talking in a

SCHOOL BUS DRIVER

*Pattengill Elementary, bus 78, 1991.
Never stop dreaming, never stop trying!*

moderate tone had the effectiveness of broken windshield wipers during monsoon season in Thailand. Suddenly, through the sounds of frenzy, little 5-year-old Sara said, "Hey, Melvin, don't have a cow. We're running for our lives!" I couldn't help but laugh out loud as I got rid of the bees with the aid of a newspaper. What could have been high adventure if this incident had occurred on the expressway was handled with ease and a little laughter.

LIFE IN THE DANGER ZONE

/Best Bus Driver Award/

Driver: Melvin

Bus #: 78

School System: Ann Arbor Public Schools

Please Come Back Next Year!

Signed: Chris

A fantastic award from one of my Pattengill students. January, 1991.

November 11, 1992

The headline in the *Ann Arbor News* read "Rage-Prone Student Barred from Pioneer." Ashanti, an 18-year-old Ann Arbor Pioneer high school student brought terror right to the doorstep of the transportation department.

September 30, 1992, started out like any other school day, but it ended like a scene out of *Boyz -N- the Hood*. Pioneer had just finished for the day when Ashanti learned his girlfriend had inadvertently left his pager on the school bus. The bus driver found it and turned it in to the transportation office. Ashanti was out of control with anger and decided to retrieve the pager by any means necessary.

He burst into the transportation office and immediately demanded his pager from the director. In typical form, she denied his vocal request. The pager would only be turned over to a school official or legal guardian. Ashanti's anger was at the boiling point, and the director was not about to give an inch. She didn't know he was raised by a grandmother because his father was incarcerated and his mother was a habitual drug user. She didn't know and didn't care. He wasn't going to get that pager.

The bald-headed, muscular football player was at his wits' end. Usually his enormous size and loud outbursts were enough to get him what he wanted, throughout his life. It didn't work this time, so he upped the ante by brandishing a pistol, threatening to shoot the defiant director. One can only imagine why she would not relinquish that stupid pager. I certainly wouldn't jeopardize one single life over such an immaterial object. The scene was at its apex when the dispatcher and several other male drivers responded. Ashanti was escorted out of the building, but not before he threatened to "blow up the place" when he returned.

The police were immediately dispatched and apprehended Ashanti in short order. Later it was discovered that the weapon he brandished was a starter pistol, unbeknownst to all the transportation employees at the time. What would have been a clear-cut suspension for any other student turned into a Perry Mason-size legal battle. Because Ashanti was classified as a special education student, state and federal laws prohibit him from being suspended for more than ten days without a court order. It literally took a court injunction by Judge Patrick J. Conlin to keep him out of school. If it were not for the court injunction, his special education status would have allowed him back in school, subsequently putting students and other school personnel at risk.

Ashanti's life first started to spiral out of control when his grandmother died in the spring of 1990. Ashanti then started shoplifting. Juvenile authorities tried to help him and his mother with counseling, but his paroxysms continued. I can only imagine how difficult it must have been for him under the tumultuous family conditions he was raised in. His mother served nine months jail time in 1988 and three weeks in 1990 after she was caught in a drug raid. Still, the safety of all students should take precedence over any student who carries a weapon and threatens violence. Ashanti was so troubled that he left his court proceedings yelling and screaming threats at the Pioneer principal, Dr. Don Jones.

The school district bent over backwards to accommodate Ashanti. They even funded and developed, pursuant to court order, a home-bound schooling program that would allow him to graduate. I strongly believe in certified home schooling alternatives for troubled youths, along with professional family intervention such as the Catholic Social Services "Friendly Gorilla" mentor program, covered later in this book.

SCHOOL BUS DRIVER

Having a good time outside the retirement party with school bus driver, Claudia Wildox, June, 1995.

Jo Anne Brown

Wednesday, March 10, 1993

"Oh, my God, a bomb!" were the words repeated throughout Slauson Middle School. Five seventh graders were suspended for bringing a pipe bomb to school. What would make teenagers do such a thing? Three of the boys were only twelve years old! If the bomb had exploded it would have sent small pieces of metal flying through the air at 2,500 feet per second. Needless to say, the carnage would have been incredible. It would have left bodies lying around like a Vietnam battlefield.

A quick-thinking teaching assistant overheard a conversation in the boys' gym locker room and informed Principal Gary Court, thus circumventing a potential tragedy. What also troubled me about this incident was that the bomb could have gone off by heat or friction. Just think of the consequences if one of the boys had the bomb on the school bus. If a pipe bomb like the one confiscated at Slauson had gone off on a school bus, sixty or more kids would have been killed along with the bus driver, causing an accident that would resemble a plane crash. I hope the students were properly disciplined! Not only did they bring a pipe bomb to school, according to news reports, police also confiscated three other bombs in the students' homes. The students risked their lives, and the lives of family members, other students, and the general public.

I was shaken to my bootstraps when I learned that accused serial bomber Ted Kaczynski received his doctorate in mathematics from Ann Arbor's University of Michigan. I was working on my last draft of this manuscript when he was arrested in April of 1996. I hope that inserting this eerie bit of autobiographical information helps in turning the young students' lives around. His arrest should send a clear message that bombs are not something to be played with.

Ann Arbor is a very fine town with an excellent school district, without question one of the best in the nation. I wouldn't live anywhere else, and would recommend it to anyone. Our district, just like any other school district, suffers from societal problems that have afflicted the whole nation. It would be nice if everything was sugar and spice, but it isn't.

To grow as a society, and a community, we must acknowledge and praise the tremendous amount of good we instill, and try to correct the problems that plague all of us. The truth in this book will be hard for a lot of people to deal with. I just hope they recognize the majority of good as the benchmark, and the hard truths as incidents to grow from.

Wednesday, September 1, 1993

It was the first day of school, with all the excitement that the start of a school year brings. Because of the lack of adequate hours available at the start of the year, I elected to sub-drive until a decent route with more working hours became available. Subs drive every day, but the job is more difficult because of the uncertainty and lack of familiarity in the routes you do.

It was early in the morning and I was driving bus 103 when the call came over the radio from K.C. His school bus was involved in a three vehicle accident on Ellsworth Road. It was one of the worst I've ever seen. The route I was driving took me near that location, and I was stunned to see what appeared to be a mangled Oldsmobile that had struck the school bus. Also involved was a sports car. I noticed a van on the side of the road, but it was hard to see if it was a part of the accident. The police department, fire department, and an ambulance were on the scene. It looked like the Mississippi. There was a river of gasoline surrounding the bus and the vehicles involved. At least one person and maybe more were rushed to the hospital.

It wasn't until later in the school year that I had an opportunity to talk with K.C. about the accident. I asked him if any of the kids were seriously injured, and if he implemented a bus evacuation drill. None of the kids were seriously injured, he told me, and he did implement a front/rear door evacuation. He said, "I told the kids front and rear door evacuation, and they were off in less than 30 seconds." K.C. then went on to tell me about the particulars of the accident and how he was hit.

Very seldom do bus drivers receive recognition for the important job that we do. You only hear about the mistakes made. And when a bus driver make a mistake

SCHOOL BUS DRIVER

it's a front page headline for you local newspaper, along with TV coverage at six o'clock. K.C. put his life on the line to make sure all of his students were off the bus safely before he departed. His calm demeanor put the kids at ease when everything around them seemed to be crashing in. For years, K.C. has transported thousands of kids safely, excelling at his profession, yet like other drivers he received little or no credit for the tremendous job he's done.

I was walking through the transportation lounge in March of 1996 when Sherri, a fellow driver, stopped me. She asked me if I would sign a card that she had for K.C. I was perplexed by her request. "I didn't know anything was wrong with K.C." Sherri responded by telling me that K.C. had been diagnosed with cancer. I hadn't seen him around but I didn't think much of it, because there was no official word that anything was amiss with him or his family.

The news was devastating. I barely managed to gather myself to sign the card. As I struggled to keep my composure, I asked Sherri if I could donate to the collection she was taking for his family. I'll always remember K.C. as a person who would take the time to talk with anybody, and he never had a caustic thing to say about anyone.

Get well soon, K.C., and thanks for he great job that you have done throughout the years. You've brought honor and integrity to our fine profession. My prayers go out to you and your family.

Friday, June 10, 1994

On the last day of school for neighboring Pinckney school district, a 12-year-old boy was hit by a school bus in front of Hiawatha Beach Church. It's every school bus driver's worst nightmare come true. Compassion fills your heart immediately for the kid. The official report listed him in critical condition at the University of Michigan hospital. When an incident like that happens, rumors as to how it occurred saturate the bus lot.

After reading about the accident in the local newspaper, the daily conversation with the food service personnel at Forsythe on June 13 took on a somber air. The unconfirmed report was that the student was inadvertently pushed during a confrontation that occurred after he got off the bus. I'm sure the driver will never be the same, because every school bus driver's first concern is for the students. Liability always hangs over you, but concern for your students is paramount. You never want to see one of your students get hurt or killed when you're driving.

June 14, 1994, 6:45 a.m.

It's my birthday, but I can't afford to take the day off. Thoughts of what I'm going to do when I get off work, and the tragic Pinckney accident, swirl through my head.

It's now 7:35 a.m., and I'm halfway through the middle school run when Mike gets on board with a grocery-size brown paper bag. With just two days of school left, what could this student have in the bag? Pranks and vandalism have always been more prevalent during the last days of school. Possibly that is a way some students vent their relief that the school year is finally over. Normally I wouldn't give a second thought to a student bringing a bag on the bus—it's just that Mike has a history of bizarre conversations.

School policy does not allow for unauthorized searches of students, so he got on the bus like all other

Logan Elementary, bus 82, 1992–93 school year. One fantastic group of kids that I really enjoyed driving!

LIFE IN THE DANGER ZONE

students throughout the year without being searched. My first thoughts were, "Relax, Melvin. He probably just has a science project in the large bag." But then I remembered the five Slauson Middle School students that were suspended for bringing a pipe bomb to school. As the ride continued I kept looking in the rear view mirror, checking, checking to make sure the bag did not play a part in possible revenge against another student. Mike was quieter than normal for that morning ride. On most days he would say such things as, "Melvin, did you shoot or kill anybody when you were in the Marine Corps?" I would say, "No, Mike, why would you ask such a thing?" Mike would then laugh and say, "Man, it would be cool to shoot someone!"

Since Mike was often a troubled student, my concern and attention were in high gear when he stepped on board with his brown paper bag. Eternity seemed closer than the end of the ride that morning. When the bus came to a stop, Mike scurried off before I could ask about the contents of the bag. He was later seen outside the recreation room. Apparently, he had some type of game inside his bag.

The ride that morning proved uneventful, thank God. School bus drivers have to be concerned with everything, no matter that it appears to be insignificant. Because of the growing violence in our society, some crime-ridden schools are required to have metal detectors, but school buses do not have such precautionary devices.

That last day of school for the Pinckney school bus driver will be the start of a life never lived before or desired. One fight, push, punch, student act of aggression, or brown paper bag could change a school bus driver's life forever.

IV

The Caretakers

Most people know their doctor, lawyer, dentist, veterinarian, aerobics instructor, and their child's school teacher. But the vast majority of the general public does not know their child's school bus driver. Knowing the bus driver can give a parent an added insight into the behavior of one's child and school activities that could result in severe problems. Kids talk openly on the bus! Sometimes drivers have firsthand knowledge of potential problems looming on the horizon for some students. When a bus driver knows a child's parent on a personal basis, he or she goes the extra mile to make sure the child gets home safely and stays out of trouble. For the majority of students, the fact that the bus driver knows the parent has a very positive impact on their bus behavior.

As caretakers, bus drivers feel the concern of every parent when we drive off to school with their precious child. We see the uncertainty in their eyes as the bus snakes its way through the neighborhood, picking up the future of families. We care, we really care about the job we do and the lives we are responsible for. We are the caretakers!

Tuesday, October 31, 1995, 4:20 p.m.

The majority of elementary students have already been taken home. Dispatch calls bus 007 about little 5-year-old Jessie Jack. Apparently Jessie didn't get off at his regular stop, unbeknownst to the substitute driver. The mother is frantic on the phone line as she tries to describe the clothing and shoes worn to school by Jessie. The dispatcher tries to soothe the mother and get more pertinent information such as Jessie's height, weight, hair color, etc.

As the mother completes the description of Jessie, suddenly she starts to feel lightheaded from all the anxiety. Abruptly she hangs up as she reaches out for the nearby chair to brace herself. After collecting all the pertinent information, the dispatch operator sends out a description of Jessie over the airwaves. Within minutes the caretakers/school bus drivers saturate the neighborhood looking for Jessie. Up and down Seventh Street more than 40 buses comb the area, as side streets resemble yellow streaks of giant vehicle humanity searching for the three feet five inches of precocious child. None of the drivers searching gave a second thought about their own family obligations; finding Jessie was the paramount concern for all the drivers, including myself.

As I rounded the bend on Sunnyside Street, onto Mount Pleasant, I noticed what appeared to be a small child with a large cardboard box on his head, wearing miniature Fila tennis shoes. His shoes and pants fit the description of little Jessie. I immediately parked the bus and approached the diminutive walking microwave-size box, with two eye holes cut out for sight. The walking box immediately stopped when my school bus approached directly across the street. I stopped, crossed the street, and asked the darting eyes through the large box, "Are you Jessie Jack?"

He lifted the box and replied, "Yes."

"Hello, Jessie, my name is Melvin. I'm a school bus driver. Please come with me. Your mother Hillary is worried about you."

We crossed the street and I radioed base, advising them that the child had been found without harm. After contacting dispatch, I asked little Jessie why he didn't come home, and why he had a box on his head.

"I wanted to get a head start on the other trick or treaters," replied Jessie.

"But why the big box, Jessie?"

He looked up in puzzlement as to why I would ask such a dumb question, then replied by saying, "I didn't want anyone to recognize me!"

Every year, school bus drivers all over the country locate lost kids, and return kids back to school when their parents don't show. We do it not just because it's our job. We do it because we care!

Tuesday, March 12, 1996

The parent conference was scheduled for 9:30 a.m. at Clague Middle School. The clock showed 9:45 before Mr. Harding walked in. He was 15 minutes late for his daughter's discipline conference, but he made no apologies for his late arrival. Waiting for him was his daughter Tonya, along with myself, Joyce the bus driver, the principal, Littlejohn, and Kelvin Dobbins, supervisor. What led up to the discipline conference were several written reports involving bus misbehavior and insubordination toward Joyce. Tonya was serving a one week suspension pending a parent conference with the principal and transportation representatives.

The conference was called to try and bring about a solution to Tonya's profane language on the bus, loud outbursts, driver disrespect, fighting, and her refusal to sit in her assigned seat. The best way to get an unconcerned parent's attention is to, as a last resort, suspend a persistently disruptive student from riding the bus until the parent shows up for a conference. I have yet to see a parent embrace transporting their child to school because of a suspension, or worse yet, welcome their company at home all day. Mr. Harding was slightly perturbed because he had to take time off from his work schedule.

Mr. Littlejohn started the conference out, but soon Kelvin took over the theme of the conversation. I could see the look in Tonya's eyes as she scanned the conference table from left to right, making a mental note of who was present. Her father sat to the right of her at the end of the table, while Mr. Littlejohn sat further down the right side of the table. Myself and Joyce were on the adjacent side, with Kelvin at the head. This was my first parent conference as a team leader since receiving the position in December of 1995. Prior to

THE CARETAKERS

being selected, I had been on the driver's side of parent conferences.

As the meeting progressed, emphasis was placed on correcting Tonya's behavior and her total lack of respect for the driver. Mr. Harding seemed surprised to see all the written reports on Tonya that had been sent home accompanied by phone calls. Tonya lived with her grandmother, who apparently handled most of the child raising responsibilities. Either the grandmother didn't bother to inform the father of his daughter's problems at school, or he simply didn't care to get involved until the problem became urgent.

Needless to say, the ball was dropped in regards to meaningful parental involvement, so crucial in early child development. Kelvin was in rare form with a "Hallmark card" performance. He dealt directly with the problems at hand with compassion for Tonya's well-being and respect for her father. His tightrope walk was flawless, and he didn't look once at John for a safety net.

As the conference grew more intense, Tonya continued to scan the room with increasing frequency. Suddenly Tonya just broke down and started crying. The enormity of the whole situation just hit her. Her actions had brought the formidable group together and the thought of so many people focused on her disruptive behavior caused her tremendous duress. I was taken aback by her sudden display of emotion. Then I looked over at Joyce. She had a look of total amazement on her face.

When the conference was over, I asked Joyce, "What was that puzzled look on your face all about?" Joyce replied by saying, "That girl in the room today was not the same person who rides my bus!" I knew exactly what she meant. So often troubled students hide behind a veil of toughness in front of their peer group as they try to keep the emotional pain they carry inside from erupting.

Later that day Tonya rode the school bus home. Within minutes of departing the bus, Tonya got in a fight with another middle school student. The fight was extremely violent, with Tonya sending the fellow Clague student to the hospital. The young lady she got into a fight with was the daughter of one of our bus drivers. The whole encounter looked like something out of the old "Dodge City." Police were called to keep a lid on the melee, but the damage had been done.

When I heard about the incident the next day at Clague, I felt awful. What more could have been done? Did Tonya succumb to the weight of living in a government-subsidized housing complex, or was the constant teen peer pressure and a dysfunctional family responsible for her violent behavior?

Approximately one month later on April 22, 1996, Tonya's little brother, Jiles, a student at nearby Thurston Elementary, was in trouble. His behavior mirrored his older sister's on elementary bus 79, despite having a different driver. Mr. Harding was again summoned to another discipline conference, this time on behalf of his son. This conference would be different than the last one. No tears would be shed or words of apology issued. The procedure would be the same: countless phone calls and letters were sent home, but to no avail. Even a call was made as a reminder of the next day's conference. Despite all efforts by the school and transportation department, Mr. Harding didn't bother to even show up or call for his son's very important conference.

It's sad to say, but I've seen so many teachers, administrators, school bus drivers, principals, etc., show more concern for troubled kids than some of their parents or guardians. Being a school bus driver is more than just transporting students from point A to point B. It's a total commitment to the welfare of all the kids that you are responsible for.

Life in the shoes of a school bus driver is filled with incredible highs that you get from daily encounters with kids. But every now and then a tragedy takes you on a ride that you would rather not go on.

This all brings me to the tragic suicide on Tuesday, April 5, 1994, of Jamey Hillegas, a student from Ann Arbor Huron High School. The story received front page headlines in the April 8, 1994 edition of the *Ann Arbor News*.

Jamey had everything most kids dream of. He was a scholar, athlete and musician. Jamey was a mathematical giant; he could do mind-twisting problems in his head when most kids would need a calculator or computer. For the last two years he had placed in the top 50 contestants in the Michigan Math Prize competition. Jamey was one of only a few winners of the National Council of Teachers of English Award after his teacher submitted a sample of his writing to a national panel. Yet all his athletic talent and metal prowess didn't stop him from shooting himself because he was not accepted by Harvard or Yale universities.

Unbelievable—all that talent wasted because he didn't get into the school of his choice, even though he *was* accepted by Cornell and Northwestern! For a week I thought about the growing escalation of teenage suicide, so I decided to ask a teenager about today's peer pressure.

It was Tuesday, April 12, 1994. I was driving route 71 and having a general conversation with Edith, a Forsythe Middle School student. She lived on Miller, and told me her father had attended Harvard. She was very familiar with the Jamey Hillegas incident, so I asked her, "Can you understand why a teenager would

SCHOOL BUS DRIVER

Mr. Kelvin Dobbins

kill himself?" To my surprise, she said yes. She then went on to say that to prevent this thing from happening, "His parents should have sat him down and told him, 'It's not the end of the world if you're not accepted by Harvard or Yale.'"

I know that advice sounds simple, but for some parents it's hard to do. Double-digit inflation demands the necessity of two incomes. Increasingly you find more and more parents absent from home. Their work day could start at 7:00 a.m. and last until 7:00 p.m. They don't have time for a brief conversation, let alone time to help their child with homework. Kids require a tremendous amount of time. You can't put in a daily 12 to 14 hour work day without some type of family repercussions.

Being a mentor is one of the single most important aspects of parenting. It requires an inordinate amount of time. There's just no short cut or easy way to accomplish it, even with the help of the caretakers.

V

Kindergarten Posse

Kindergartners are in a class all by themselves. There is no other age group with their curiosity, candor, demeanor, or sense of humor. When driving kindergartners, you have to pay special attention when transporting eight or more kids, and in cases of ten or more the services of a monitor should be mandatory. It's their first year of school, and the school bus resembles a big playhouse to them. But what might be acceptable behavior to them could spell disaster on the bus. Parents in many cases don't prepare them for the trip on the ten-ton vehicle. Playing with windows, the emergency door, the escape hatch, running, standing, and horseplay are safety concerns that should be addressed before the little ones ride.

The kindergarten portion of route 50 in November, 1993, only lasted one and a half hours, but it was filled with spontaneity, humor, and sincerity that only a driving experience with kindergartners can bring. Charlie was a very bright kindergartner with the wit of a person twice his age. His curiosity was sparked when I started sub-driving after the temporary loss of his second bus driver, who contracted cancer. His first bus driver was terminated in the first round of drug testing.

SCHOOL BUS DRIVER

He got caught and the punishment was swift—one strike and he was out!

Charlie's opening round of questions started with, "Where is Butch?" when he first laid eyes on me.

"Well, Butch is not driving school buses anymore."

"So he quit!"

"Well, I guess you could say that, Charlie, but don't worry. I am a very good bus driver. In fact, you could say I'm number one, ha, ha, ha."

"You're not number one, Butch is number one. You're number zero!" Every day thereafter for about two weeks, Charlie referred to me as "number zero" when he boarded the bus.

I was starting to feel pretty dejected when I thought I'd try some reverse psychology on the little guy. So after continuous bombardment by Charlie, I gave in and said, "No, I'm not number one—you are!"

He had a look of befuddlement on his face and said, "So you give up, huh?"

"Yes, Charlie, I give up—you're number one."

Then Charlie replied, "You know, when I say you're number zero, I really don't hate you. I really like you—I just say that because I really do like you. You're not number zero, you are number one!"

I acknowledged Charlie with a polite "thank you" and continued the ride speechless, reflecting with awe and amazement on someone so young.

After my humbling experience with Charlie, it gave me great pleasure to witness another kindergartner leave him speechless. That person came in the form of Lindsay, three feet nine inches, dark hair, and brown eyes. Charlie was good with the one-two verbal punch combination, but he got floored by Lindsay. It was on a cold November morning when Lindsay broke tradition and sat in the middle portion of the bus, instead of the rear section with Charlie. I thought it was odd, but didn't pay much attention until Charlie yelled from the rear, "Lindsay, why aren't you sitting back here with us?" Lindsay, without turning around, said, "I want to keep this hat on my head, and you will take it off if I sit in the back." Charlie was speechless for the rest of the trip home.

I always made it a point to let my younger riders know that they were safe from bullies, verbal abuse, and "bad people" when they rode my bus. They knew that I would make it as safe as humanly possible for them, to and from school. I also made it a point to try and put their parents at ease by informing them that school bus transportation is one of the safest forms of mass transportation, according to national highway safety statistics.

On November 12, 1993, Charlie was late getting on the bus. When he finally showed up I reminded him that a number two bus driver or below would not have waited for him, and that proves that I'm number one. Charlie then started scratching his head and said, "You know why I was late?"

"No, Charlie, why were you late?"

"I was in there battling the werewolf."

I had to wait several minutes before I could start the ride home. The laughter was overwhelming.

SCHOOL BUS DRIVER

Route 71 in the 1993–1994 school year was one that I will long remember. I'm used to transporting 55 to 65 students per bus trip on a daily basis with my usual aplomb. I was assigned to route 71 because rout 50 driver, Kathy, returned after her successful bout against cancer. My four years of experience as a school bus driver had prepared me for just about any potential incident, but it was still quite a surprise when I started transporting the approximately 23 kindergartners from the Scio Farms trailer park in the western portion of Ann Arbor.

Every parent, preschool teacher, and child care provider knows that just watching 23 kids is a formidable task. Add driving a ten-ton vehicle with kindergartners unrestrained by the use of seat belts (most buses have none) through city traffic with no monitor, and you have an "Excedrin P.M." day. Although I love kids very much, they still challenge me daily. After my pleasant experience with Charlie and the rest of the kids from bus 50, it still came as a surprise when I encountered Doug S.

Doug S. was another bright kindergartner, with a mother sent from heaven. A school bus driver can almost immediately tell which parents take an active role in raising their children, and Doug's mother was one of them, one who has done a great job. A driver can tell by the way a child acts on the bus if that child has someone that cares. The student who misbehaves on the bus usually reflects problems from home in about 90 percent of the cases.

Conversations with Doug S. went like this.
"Hey, bus driver!"
"Yes, Doug."
"This bus has an awfully big steering wheel."
"You're right, Doug. The steering wheel is much bigger than your mother's van."

KINDERGARTEN POSSE

Kindergartners from left to right: Charlie, Vincent (with the hood), Alex, Lindsay, and John. 1993–94.

"Don't you get tired trying to steer that big steering wheel?"

"No, you get used to it, but the bumpy ride wears you down a little after a long day."

"Don't you get tired trying to park this big bus in your driveway and at the mall?"

"Well, Doug, I'm not allowed to drive the bus home or to the mall. We have two big parking lots at the transportation department for all the buses, near the Briarwood Mall. Do you know where that is?"

Doug nods his head yes, then starts singing a rap song by Snoop Doggy Dog. The lyrics were horrible.

"Doug, does your mother know you sing songs like that?"

"No, I heard it from one of my brother's friends and on 96.3 jams."

SCHOOL BUS DRIVER

Kindergartners from left to right: Jared, Kayle, Lauren. Wines Elementary, bus 50. Fantastic kids with great parents. 1993–94.

"Well, Doug, I think that we should tell your mother."

"Aren't you being a little overly sensitive?"

"No, Doug, not at all," I said, but inwardly I thought, "Oh no, another adult in a kindergartner's body."

After we reported the incident to Doug's mother, I was pleasantly surprised to get a hand-written apology from Doug the next day he rode. His mother made him write it out several times before he submitted his final

KINDERGARTEN POSSE

Yours truly with the kindergarten posse, left to right: Doug P., Thomas Lee, Tucker, Doug S., Tiffany, Chad, Christina, Nikka. Abbot Elementary bus 71, 1994.

draft. It was only the second time that I had a parent administer discipline in that manner.

The first time came in the 1990–1991 school year when I was driving an elementary run out of Wines School, when Mark B. flipped the middle finger sign to students on board after he departed. His parents were very upset and they made Mark write a letter of apology.

I have mentioned these two minor incidents in my book because they are good examples of how parents

SCHOOL BUS DRIVER

Reinhart

RECD OCT 21 1993
*Pride in Our Community
Leadership in Real Estate Services*

10/14/93

To Whom It May Concern:

Melvin D. Latnie who drives Bus #50 on the afternoon run for Wines School, comes highly recommended to be the pernament driver for that route. Melivin is a kind and conscientious driver, and the kids all enjoy having him as their bus driver.

Sincerley

cc: Melvin Latnie
    File

the Charles Reinhart Co. Realtors

The ultimate in job satisfaction is to be appreciated by the parents. Thank you very much, Lisa. Kayla and Lauren were great!

KINDERGARTEN POSSE

and guardians should handle their young children. Doug and Mark are two great kids with exceptional parents. Immediate parental involvement, along with other disciplinary measures, sent a message that resulted in no other bus-related problems.

Most parents really, truly care about their kids. But some parents live in a constant state of denial when their child gets into trouble, instead of addressing the problem head on. Then you have the other side of the spectrum, those who simply don't care if their child shoots, stabs, or fights someone. They don't even care if their child drops out of school altogether. When a driver knows the parent, he or she makes a conscious effort to watch out for that child—even more so when they know that parent cares.

Bad Melvin
&
the
K.G. POSSE

SCHOOL BUS DRIVER

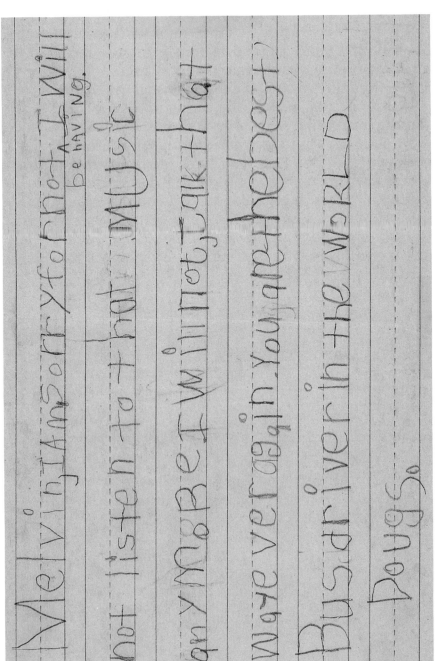

Melvin I am sorry for not behaving. I will not listen to that MUSIC any more. I will not talk that way ever agin. You are the best Bus driver in the world.

Doug S.

Fantastic letter from kindergartner Doug S. Bus 71, May 1994.

VI

The Good, Bad and Ugly

The Good: School bus drivers' concerns mirror that of the general population. We care about job security, violence, war, good education for our children, and the moral decline of America. Subjects of special interest to us, like the incident that happened to one of our drivers on January 13, 1994, always bring out the best dialogue. On that January afternoon, school bus driver Leon Bryant drove right into a potential life and death situation. He was in the middle of his afternoon run at approximately 3:00 p.m. when he came across two Slauson Middle School students, male and female, having an argument while walking home. Suddenly the girl pulled out a big kitchen knife and tried to stab the male student.

What should someone do after coming upon a life or death situation with students on the bus? Leon kept his cool and radioed base, apprising dispatch of the conflict. Dispatch notified the police, and Leon then abandoned his bus and talked the girl into surrendering her knife. This incident had a happy ending with nobody getting seriously injured, thank God. Leon put his life on the line. He, or one of the two students, could have easily lost their lives on that January day.

SCHOOL BUS DRIVER

School bus drivers are always confronted with emergencies, such as vehicle collisions, student medical problems, and physical altercations. Kids are becoming more and more aggressive. The traditional family structure is almost in ruins, with single black mothers now heading over 60 percent of their families. Fathers of all nationalities are becoming increasingly absent. Kids are seeking their teenage peers as surrogate role models, along with television. No longer can drivers count on students being innocuous.

The Bad: Lost in the uproar of the day was an incident that happened on bus 80 thirty minutes later. Kevin W., a sub-driver, reported that students were in the back section of the bus trying to set it on fire with matches. Quick thinking by Kevin averted another possible tragedy.

The role of a school bus driver is changing. That's why I strongly urge the use of video cameras on school buses. Some schools are already using them with tremendous success. Cameras have proven to be very effective in eliminating violence in and around the bus. The fear of parents witnessing their behavior has made problem students become model students.

The Ugly: The one issue that is talked about between drivers, parents, and the media more than anything else is "School bus driver leaves child on bus." How a driver could leave a student on the bus and return to the bus lot is beyond my comprehension. At minimum, a driver should check his or her bus at the school after the morning, noon, and afternoon runs. I double-check my bus after dropping off at each school and before returning to the lot.

December 7, 1992

We had a driver and monitor leave a preschooler on their bus. The child was found helplessly wandering around the massive lower bus parking lot by another driver. It was a parent's worst nightmare come true. Other school districts locally and nationally have experienced this same unfortunate blunder. After the dust settled, both ladies were suspended for at least a month. They were lucky they didn't lose their jobs. What excuse did they have? There was no excuse for being lazy and not caring. I am extremely happy that nothing serious happened to the little girl. It was an unfortunate incident that left me ashamed of my school district, because school bus drivers are in a constant battle for respectability. Although there is no excuse for this blunder, it does not reflect the majority of the fine school bus drivers that the school district of Ann Arbor has.

Tuesday, January 18, 1994

Five days after Leon Bryant had his life-threatening experience with the two Slauson student, the day was bitterly cold with the wind-chill factor at 40 below zero. Everybody was angry that Ann Arbor Public Schools were not closed. Neighboring school districts Milan, Brighton, Howell, Pinckney, and Hartland were all closed. The cold was so intense that the defrost system could not keep up. When I opened the bus door, cold air would freeze on the inside of the window every time I made a stop. Subsequently, I literally had to scrape the inside of the window with an ice scraper every time the vehicle stopped, making for a very dangerous situation because visibility was next to zero.

Drivers were calling in at an alarming rate with stranded buses. When the mechanics would come upon a disabled bus they would change the frozen fuel filters and within minutes they would freeze again. Brewer's, a local towing company, made a fortune off the Ann Arbor school district that day. I stopped counting towed buses when the number reached five. All of a sudden, my body became very tense after hearing the radio call of Kim, bus 28, at approximately 8:15 a.m. Her voice was very shaky, and it sounded as if she was delirious. The icy, deplorable road conditions had claimed another driver as a victim. It was the second such day in January when the superintendent should have called off school, the first being on January 6, 1994, when the district was hit with 11 inches of snowfall. Antwaun on bus 13 and Al on bus 103 were the victims of bus accidents that day—a day when nothing with wheels could move safely.

Kim was involved in a bad accident on westbound M-14, attempting to make a lane change on the icy freeway. Her bus destroyed the vehicle it collided with.

THE GOOD, BAD AND UGLY

Yes sir... No sir... yes sir you're absolutely right sir there is no need for a snow day!!

Now that that is over....

Our dispatcher asked her twice if she was okay. She replied both times that there were no injuries, but her voice sounded otherwise. I was saying to myself, "Get somebody to the accident, please don't let there be any kids hurt or killed, let Kim be all right, hurry, hurry. . . ." Kim was all right and there were no injuries to the kids or the other driver. After the police report and the mandatory accident report that every driver has to fill out regardless of fault, Kim then had to go and take a drug test because the accident was so severe it required at least one vehicle being towed.

Superintendents and administrators who are responsible for canceling school when the weather is extreme should be more sensitive to the harmful effects that driving in inclement weather could have.

The next day Detroit Public Schools made the same

SCHOOL BUS DRIVER

From left to right, Diane, Michael, and Nicole.

mistake that our district made on Tuesday, and it almost cost a child his life. Little 9-year-old Darrin Harvey was in school despite the 60-below wind-chill factor. Darrin's mother was four minutes late picking him up when he decided to walk home, a little more than a mile. Darrin was just minutes into his walk home when he was overcome by the killer cold. No one would help the black child as his little body lay frozen on the snow-covered ground. His little hand was reaching for help when, by the grace of God, 71-year-old Rush Yarnell came to his rescue.

When Mr. Yarnell arrived, Darren's little body was already in shock and his hands were frostbitten and white. According to reports, his school book was lying next to him, and one shoe was completely off. His hands were outstretched as if begging for help.

Little Darrin survived this life-threatening ordeal, but the medical technician that treated him told Mr. Yarnell that Darrin was just ten minutes away from death. Any kid that has to wait at a school bus stop could have been exposed to the same ordeal that Darrin experienced. I'm sending this plea to all superintendents reading this book: stop the foolishness and cancel school in severe weather. No one can replace a life, and no reason is good enough to jeopardize students!

VII

No to Privatization

Just about every school district, small business, and corporation is seeking ways to save money. At the top of just about everyone's list are job layoffs. Rather than looking at viable ways of reducing costs without job loss, districts, like businesses, elect job reductions first. The Ann Arbor school district has also looked into the process of bus privatization, like nearby Pinckney school district and other districts across the country.

Although it appears as of this writing that Pinckney will make the catastrophic decision to implement private services, Ann Arbor has, for the moment, chosen not to privatize after getting an unfavorable report from Laidlaw, a nationally-known private company that specializes in school takeovers for profit. If there is no possibility of profit, they're not interested. School districts fail to realize that when they give control over to a private company, they give up just about all their decision-making powers, making it impossible for parents, teachers, the school board, and administrators to plan an effective curriculum for students. Also lost in the transition is control over goods and services, virtu-

SCHOOL BUS DRIVER

ally making the old administrators and parents impotent in regard to students' welfare.

Ann Arbor is unique because the district covers 125 square miles of territory with about 130 to 140 drivers. Preschoolers, kindergartners, elementary, middle school, high school, and a fair amount of physically challenged students receive service. The total number of students that ride is approximately 7,000 out of 15,000 attending school. 2,500 private school students also receive transportation. According to 1995 Ann Arbor Public Schools figures:

- School media specialists help students check out over 18,000 books each week.

- Cafeteria workers serve 6,800 meals to students each day.

- Each day, teachers of English as a second language (ESL) work with 560 K–12 and 400 adult education students who are from more than 50 countries and who speak 47 different languages.

- Adult education teachers will assist 152 students in completing their high school education this year.

- High school counselors help students complete 1,850 applications for college each year.

- School nurses are responsible for caring for and following up on 2,200 students each year.

- Teacher consultants help 700 students with special learning needs each year.

- Each day, custodians and maintenance workers maintain 600 acres of lawn and grounds, as well as clean and tend over 3 million square feet of space in 42 buildings.

NO TO PRIVATIZATION

- Child care workers supervise and provide programs for 1,000 children before and after school each day.

- Paraprofessionals provide supplemental instruction, supervision, and tutoring for over 10,000 students each year.

- Secretaries and clerical employees provide service to 15,000 students and parents, plus teachers, administrators, etc., throughout all areas of the school district (1996 estimate).

Needless to say, our district is no "mom and pop" operation. According to Gava L. Graham, transportation consultant, for the Washtenaw Intermediate school district, "If the Ann Arbor school district decided to privatize, it's not because it's more cost effective, but because they choose to." Gava told me those words on February 22, 1994 at 4:30 p.m. after I asked her directly about the possibility of privatization. Every year, our department closes the year "in the black" because of the revenue gained from field trips, comparatively low wages, minimum health care, and sound fiscal management. The school district could be even more financially sound if it reduced the wholesale loss of bus drivers each year.

There are several reasons why we and other large districts around the state lose so many drivers:

1) The requirements are extensive, despite the insufficient hours and pay received. A commercial drivers license, first aid and CPR, basic school bus driver training, advanced bus driver training, drug testing, excellent driving record, and certificate of continuing driver education are just some of our district's requirements.

SCHOOL BUS DRIVER

2) Management loves to "stockpile" drivers when they can because they can shorten normally eight-hour routes into four-hour routes, thus limiting potential overtime, working hours, and their payout on health benefits. This practice is financial hard on drivers, causing them to quit or not return for the next school year.

3) In Michigan, the majority of drivers are only offered seasonal work because of the long student summer vacation. This practice is not only bad on morale, but it also exposes the public to less experienced drivers each and every year, from the high turnover.

If a private company came in, they would reduce wages even more and eliminate health care benefits altogether. This action would make it impossible for them to find competent drivers, thus putting our most precious resource, children, and the general public at risk.

Then how can the school district save money?

I submitted a letter to the former transportation director as well as the present school superintendent on May 5, 1994. In the letter I listed some of the following proposals: the best way to maximize savings is to utilize your assets and reduce operating costs. School bus drivers are assets that are not used to the fullest. For the past seven years I have witnessed schools such as Pioneer High, Huron High, Clague Middle School, Logan Elementary, etc., hire private tour bus companies for school field trips.

One of the main reasons teachers repeatedly give for this use of tour buses is comfort. We lose thousands of dollars each year because our district does not have a tour bus with such amenities as air conditioning, seats

NO TO PRIVATIZATION

Mr. Mark Spears, former school bus driver and tour bus operator.

that recline, a premium sound system, etc. The ride on a new or old school bus can at times feel like riding a bucking bronco. I investigated the feasibility of purchasing a tour bus with Mark Spears, a former school bus driver and tour operator, teachers that have paid for field trips, and other drivers. We all came up with the same conclusion. Adding a tour bus would pay for itself in one year, and any year thereafter would be profit. Also, the addition of a tour bus would increase business from nonprofit companies. For years we have transported nonprofit companies and organizations on trips for a competitive fee under the present board-ap-

SCHOOL BUS DRIVER

A tour bus like the one that Mark Spears drives would bring in the big bucks. School bus drivers are already licensed to drive tour buses.

proved agreement. The addition of one or two tour buses would dramatically increase the revenue of any district from nonprofit organizations.

Reiterating the letter submitted to the former director, Ann Arbor has some of the best school bus drivers in the world, who are automatically qualified to drive tour buses. The additional work and revenue could be used to help retain drivers, thus increasing productivity and lowering operating expenses.

Another way to increase revenue would be to expand the school bus repair shop, or establish a second repair site altogether. It would allow the garage supervisor and his first-class mechanics the ability to service outside school districts' buses for profit. By increasing the service bay area by just two, the profits would be staggering. School districts around the country are retaining their fleets of buses for a longer period of time.

NO TO PRIVATIZATION

Our garage supervisor confirmed that he is inundated with repair requests from other districts and private businesses that he cannot fulfill because of regulations and a lack of adequate manpower and facilities. Presently the Ann Arbor school district is in the business of child care and selling lunches for other than student consumption. Why not expand the garage? There is a lot more money to be made in it.

A multi-million dollar savings could also come from requiring students to buy their own musical instruments and renting the instruments presently owned by the public schools. I talked to the deputy superintendent shortly after submitting my letter. He said that some of my ideas were very good and he would pass them along to the school board. As of July 1994, nothing had changed.

Another very important reason not to privatize busing is traffic. If a private company takes over a school district, they will more than likely eliminate high school transportation. When you eliminate high school transportation, it forces thousands (depending on the size of the district) of additional cars driven by teenagers onto the roads during peak work hours. The traffic jams would make daily commuting a nightmare in the fall, and a horror show in the winter with the snow and ice. Also, schools would have to increase parking dramatically. Cities would have to expand, widen, and generate more revenue for the maintenance of city streets. Also, 14-year-olds would be eligible to declare hardship and obtain a minor's driving permit, a "hardship license," under 1996 Michigan law. If you think 16-year-olds are bad drivers, just imagine 14-year-olds on the road! The carnage could be incredible.

If you don't believe in such an outcome, visit the Brighton, Michigan area school district. Brighton, because of budget problems, eliminated high school bus service and it resulted in nothing short of gridlock. In August 1994, the small school district received over 200 complaint calls in just two days. The district also made another monumental mistake by acquiring a new two million dollar transportation center that now collects dust. The answer lies not in selling your assets, but using them as the valuable resources that they really are.

NO TO PRIVATIZATION

Transportation Department: upper parking lot.

Transportation Department: lower parking lot.

VIII

Special Education

The subject of privatization brings out strong arguments for and against when brought up in a public forum. But it pales in comparison when the subject of special education is broached. The mere discussion of cutting special education costs brings outrage and accusations that people lack compassion. But the fact still remains that in the state of Michigan, special education costs have doubled in the last ten years alone. Why? The State of Michigan pays for services for the disabled until they turn 27, despite federal law only requiring services up to age 21. In Washtenaw County alone there are 5,323 students that are labeled special education, and the numbers are growing. Washtenaw Intermediate School District alone spends 25.14 million dollars on special education, according to 1995 statistics published in the February 25, 1995 edition of the *Ann Arbor News*. That figure does not include what neighboring school districts are paying, nor the cost for special education students in the inclusion programs at public schools.

SCHOOL BUS DRIVER

New York, in 1995, spent $22,000 per physically challenged student, compared to just $5,000 per student in general education. That comes to more than four times the amount the average student gets allocated for education. Add into the equation Michigan's age 27 commitment for disabled students, and what you have is an expense that cripples programs such as art, music, sports, busing, gym, tutoring, field trips, etc., especially for smaller school districts that don't have the tax base to fully support both general education and special education students. When it comes to cuts, general education students have taken severe hits, time and time again.

Is it just or fair for this type of inequity to continue? The lack of money for general education students in the Kalkaska school district, located in northern Michigan, resulted in the district closing school early and eliminating vital services such as bus transportation and after-school activities. Many other school districts across the nation are experiencing similar financial problems.

Don't get me wrong—I have nothing but compassion for anyone with legitimate physical or mental deficiencies. But should we continue to increase our tax burden and reduce services, when we could save millions of dollars by conforming to the more than adequate national requirement of age 21, or at least age 25, for disabled students?

Monumental savings could come from minor cuts in special education and other programs that I have enumerated throughout this book. We aren't talking about nickels and dimes here! Millions of dollars could go toward the betterment of *all students* by cutting and expanding programs. Action has to be taken to save our public schools. It is my sincere hope that this book will inspire others to get involved in saving and improving our public schools.

IX

Baggy Pants!

February 9, 1995, 6:50 a.m.

Winter cold grips Ann Arbor with a vengeance. As I approach the Packard and Hikone stop on my high school run, I notice Jimmy running up Hikone Drive in the distant background. He is running late, with a full set of books in one hand and his baggy pants in the other. Mighty Morphin Power Rangers are the rage for elementary kids, and baggy pants, ten sizes too large with no belt, are the fashion statement of middle school and high school students.

Jimmy, like the typical rap artist, has his on, along with the designer matching boxer shorts that boys showcase by securing their belt (when they wear one) below butt level. Jimmy is running toward the bus, waving desperately, trying to get my attention before I pull off. Then suddenly Jimmy goes airborne, books flying like they were launched from a catapult. His pants had dropped around his ankles when he waved for the last time, entangling his feet like a roped calf at a rodeo show. You could hear the "thud" sound when his body came to rest. Shocked and amazed, I called out, "Are you okay?"

SCHOOL BUS DRIVER

After a brief pause, Jimmy said, "I've fallen, and I can't get up!" He sounded like the elderly lady on the First Alert home alarm commercial.

Responding, I said, "Don't move. I'll help you out."

"No, no, no, just continue," blurted Jimmy as he lay in a human star position. Later he told me why he had insisted that I continue. The concrete tore a large hole in his boxer shorts, exposing more of his bottom than his baggy pants!

X

Discipline

When I was a teenager attending North Junior High in Belleville, Michigan, students were paddled by the principal, then suspended without hesitation if they violated school rules in such ways as fighting, drug possession, carrying weapons, etc. Now in 1997, if a principal uses that same type of discipline, he or she could face lawsuits that could end his or her career. At one time, parents would actually thank the principal for spanking their child and invite him or her over for dinner. Not any more. If a principal uses spanking for discipline, in the majority of public schools that person couldn't sleep at night for fear of being shot by the parent the next day in retaliation—despite the parents' ineptness to administer discipline themselves.

Members of our society repeatedly say the times are different now. Time-outs and passive dialogue are considered the model approach for raising just about all kids today. Kids know this kind of discipline is standard procedure and take full advantage of it, while teenage violence is at an all-time high. Not all kids need severe punishment as a form of discipline; a good portion of them fully get the message of their wrongdoing by the consequences of their deeds. But for an increasing percentage of teenagers, more than just talking is needed.

The times are not different now; it's the people that are radically changing. Growing segments in society glamorize single parents such as Murphy Brown and the love of the almighty dollar the 1980s brought about. No longer important are God, families, morality, ethics, and the crucial part fathers play in the upbringing of sons and daughters. Television is now the standard child-rearing nanny used in many fractured families.

And the children are the ones that suffer, according to David Blankenhorn, author of *Fatherless America*. In married-couple homes with preschool children, median family income in 1992 was approximately $41,000. In single-mother homes with young children, median income was about $9,000—a ratio of more than four to one. Of all married-couple families in the nation in 1992, about six percent lived in poverty; of all female-headed families, about 35 percent lived in poverty—a ratio of almost six to one.

In the 1950s, two-parent families were the norm. During that time, crime, teenage pregnancies, drug use, suicides, and violence were minuscule at best. The 1990s have brought us record-breaking crime, poverty, drug use, disruptive behavior, and a growing number of kids that are totally out of control. As bus drivers we come into contact with them everyday.

Our society has become so lacking in morality that we even legally allow single females to give birth to kids that are conceived by artificial insemination. We care so much for the biological rights of single mothers that we totally lose sight of the "head job" the kid will go through not knowing who his or her father is!

It is hard enough for an intact nuclear family to raise kids successfully, let alone a single mother raising children without knowledge of their father. Author

DISCIPLINE

Peter L. Berger on models of human relationships finds that, "One of the single most archaic functions of society is to take away from individuals the burden of choice." Kids desperately need, if at all possible, two active parents in their lives on a daily basis, not weekend or monthly, to actively fulfill the gift of parenting.

The decline of married, two-parent, male and female families can be directly linked to the increase in crime, poverty, drug use, welfare, etc., according to David Blankenhorn and other known societal scholars. The majority of males in prison, at some point in their life, has dropped out of the educational system or has experienced breakup in the family structure, or both. A great majority of them also come from extremely dysfunctional families. You can see early signs of trouble by age six or seven, according to some teachers.

People in our society no longer accept responsibility for their actions. We embrace a faultless society that does not require responsibility for our actions, then we raise kids that do not accept responsibility for theirs. True discipline must be consistent in its expectations and implementation.

For example, all one has to do is look at the infamous 1990 South Carolina case of 14-year-old Gina Grant. Gina brutally murdered her mother by repeatedly pounding her head with a lead crystal candlestick until it resembled something out of a *Friday the 13th* movie. Because she was considered a juvenile, Gina only received six months in a juvenile center, despite collaborating with her petty-thief boyfriend to make the killing look like a suicide by sticking a knife in her dead mother's neck and then placing her hand around it.

Gina's mother never beat her, according to all newspaper accounts. Gina's mother's only fault was that she was an alcoholic. The judge sympathized with Gina and sent a message to all kids of reading age. "Kill your mother or father for just six months of detention!"

Later, when Gina turned 21, she was accepted into Harvard College, then was rejected when someone mailed a newspaper clipping of her crime to the school. Students at Harvard protested in support of Gina, and even the president of Boston College requested that Gina apply to Boston College where she would assuredly be accepted. An alarming number of people gave Gina an unworthy "no fault pass" for murdering a drunken mother who couldn't even defend herself. The criminal justice system set a bad example. Some teenagers looked on this case and said, "Wow, I can kill my parents for only six months of detention and become a hero in the process." Remarkably, during the whole celebration of Gina Grant, no one burned a candle for the ultimate victim of this brutal crime, her mother. Faultless crimes don't exist. Lessons in discipline must be taught early, and repeatedly shown by your actions as concerned adults in every walk of life.

DISCIPLINE

Everyday discipline, or the lack thereof, plays a daily role in the arduous task of being a school bus driver. I love my job, as many do, but the job is made more difficult by the lack of support by some elementary principals and parents of troubled kids. The majority of drivers will confirm that the elementary portion is the most stressful and challenging segment of the job. For example, during the 1994-1995 school year, while driving route 79, there was one particular third grader that helped keep the aspirin companies in business. He was approximately four feet one inch tall with dark hair, a chubby kid with a voice reminiscent of Froggy from *The Little Rascals*.

Froggy, on a daily basis, gave me and just about every student on the bus mid-afternoon nightmares. I love kids, especially the direct honesty that they bring to our daily lives, but Froggy was a pain. Froggy lived in the Arrowwood Cooperative, a government-subsidized apartment complex on Pontiac Trail. Froggy had problems, there's no question about that, but he wasn't the only kid with special difficulties on my bus. My particular route was often referred to as the "special ed bus" because of the inordinately high amount of problem students riding. Inclusion of problem students was supposed to be evenly distributed throughout the district, but in the case of bus route 79, that policy was not adhered to.

What compounded the problems with Froggy was the persistent parental denial, the "not my kid" attitude, and the "laissez-faire," lenient "Dr. Spock lecture series" discipline applied by the elementary school principal. As of April 1995, Froggy had received nine written reports that covered at least 64 bus infractions for fighting, exposing himself, profanity directed at the bus driver, kicking, spitting, profanity directed at sev-

SCHOOL BUS DRIVER

eral students, instigating fights, screaming at the top of his lungs, uncontrollable fits, etc.

Froggy, during his reign of terror, only received one suspension for approximately five days total during an eight month rollercoaster ride. He openly talked about how he "hated school and riding the bus." His sole intention was to get kicked out of school and off the bus. In the process he displayed the most opprobrious demeanor toward myself and other adults in the position of authority. Sometimes his behavior was so obtuse it bordered on the bizarre. One day for no apparent reason he threatened to expose his penis to a little girl on the bus.

He had unzipped his pants when the girl screamed for my attention. I quickly pulled the bus over to the side of the road. Froggy then rolled over on his stomach trying to cover up the fact that his pants were unzipped. His actions created an incredible disturbance on the bus, and could have resulted in a fatal collision.

Numerous counseling sessions were fruitless with Froggy. Froggy's father was not a whole lot better; he always seemed too busy to properly address the problems of his kid. Instead of dealing with the issues at hand, he took the easy way out and blamed the school district for his son's problems. They say you can tell a tree by the fruit it bears—nothing could be more appropriate in the case of Froggy's father!

There had to be problems at home the transportation department and school were not privy to. Through his actions, Froggy desperately wanted his father to spend more time with him. He loved those rare occasions when his dad had to make the 20 minute round trip with him in tow. That was 20 minutes of attention he didn't normally get on an average TV day. But his dad hated it; he hated having to transport his kid during that brief suspension. It was so therapeutic watch-

DISCIPLINE

ing this transformation from afar. Froggy loved having his dad take him to school, but his dad hated it and fought like the devil to get him back on the bus. The principal, not wanting to inconvenience Froggy Sr., returned Froggy each and every time to the bus, creating chaos and discord, and jeopardizing the safety of all the other students riding. That kid screamed for love and attention from his father, but the only thing he got was a kick in the pants and an unwanted bus ride home.

During Froggy's frequent temper tantrums, the other kids watched intently, sometimes emulating Froggy's actions. They knew nothing would happen to them because nothing happened to Froggy. They figured the worst that could happen would be a conversation on the principal's lecture series. They witnessed Froggy run amuck without serious consequences and swear at me with no regard or respect. His actions and the passive response from the principal were creating anarchy on the bus. The elementary principal had the last word on discipline, and he repeatedly resisted any form of strong punishment. Froggy's actions deserved at least a 30 day suspension with weekly evaluations. But the principal kept him on the bus, creating a potentially explosive atmosphere.

Several elementary principals that I've come across are intimidated by parents; they fear inconveniencing them despite the misbehavior of their kids. When they repeatedly return disruptive kids to the bus, it only fuels the highly charged atmosphere that 65 kids of different grades bring to the daily bus ride.

During this whole process, the driver feels total frustration and an inordinate amount of additional stress. Our transportation employee handbook says on page 10, section 14, "The bus driver is in charge and shall assume responsibility at all times." If I as the bus driver

SCHOOL BUS DRIVER

shall assume "all responsibility," why can't I decide what type of discipline under school district rules should be applied? Yet the ultimate decision rests with the school principal.

Can you imagine calling a police officer to a civil disturbance—a fight—and having him or her tell you he or she can't do anything until his or her supervisor reviews the seriousness of this knot you have on the top of your head! We have to have eight or ten documented incidents before something can be done, but you can review my numerous reports on file at your convenience.

That's exactly how many drivers feel when they don't get support. We are dealing with an increasingly violent society that allows its kids and irresponsible parents to go unpunished for their lack of supervision and responsibility. When I was writing this segment of the book, an article in the Sunday, April 9, 1995 *Ann Arbor News* reported vandals shooting out windows at local Huron High School with a .38 caliber or 9 mm handgun and a .410 shotgun. Somewhere down the line you can bet those individuals' childhood actions, like Froggy's, went unchecked.

What is the solution? Discipline would increase tenfold if the parents were held more accountable. One of the first things we should do is to make parents ultimately responsible for their kids. I have found that parents who take an active role in parenting don't have a problem with this concept. It's the parents who don't give a damn that raise hell when discipline is applied because they have failed at their job.

In Silverton, Oregon, parents and guardians are held legally responsible for the actions of their kids. Silverton is a small town with a population of about 5,732. In January 1995, an ordinance went into effect that said parents or guardians of minors can be

DISCIPLINE

charged with a criminal offense of "failure to supervise." Depending on the infraction, parents could be ordered to attend parenting classes, pay fines of $100 to $1,000, and pay restitution up to $2,500.

This program is so successful that cities all over the nation have shown serious interest. Even San Francisco, New York, and Tokyo have looked into implementing this ordinance. And guess what? The people of Silverton love the ordinance and think it's long overdue. Parents and police chief Randy Lunsford call the program early intervention. We desperately need this program in Detroit, Ann Arbor, Ypsilanti, and other cities across this nation.

Another solution for decreasing problems on the school bus would be to let the bus driver decide the punishment of the disruptive students. If you are going to make the driver "assume all responsibility," he or she should have a hand in the final discipline decision. If that is too much power for the principal or transportation department to yield, then they should release the driver of "all responsibility" and assume any and all responsibility themselves. Just think about it: by changing the policy you instantly change the attitude of all principals.

In Mark Gerson's book *In the Classroom*, he states, "When students trust their teachers and administrators and are confident that strictly enforced rules advance a valuable learning process, discipline becomes natural, even the norm." I wholeheartedly agree with that statement. But before trust can be gained, rules and consequences must be established. A student must fear the repercussions of his or her acts over the urge to commit adolescent misbehavior.

In extreme cases, you run across a child who is in need of intensive care, at risk of being lost permanently to the ills of society. That's when you need the help of a

SCHOOL BUS DRIVER

"Friendly Gorilla." What is a Friendly Gorilla? I was scouring through the newspaper when I came across an article about a Catholic Social Services program by that name. Outside of Ann Arbor, the program targets troubled youths and gives them a surrogate male role model, someone who accompanies them everywhere they go, from sun-up to sundown. When the troubled youth wakes up in the morning and gets ready for school, the Friendly Gorilla is there. The Gorilla escorts him to school riding the same bus. He waits outside the classroom, or assists the teacher if needed. He even spends lunch and recess with the young person, and escorts him home. His days starts with the Friendly Gorilla and ends with him. During this whole interaction the Gorilla teaches, establishes friendship and trust, discipline when needed, and listens astutely.

The key to discipline starts and ends with parents or guardians. Kids will live up to the expectations you establish if you are firm and consistent.

XI

The Unspeakable Crime

About ten years ago, a friend of mine was raped. She never really fully recovered despite years of therapy she went through. It's horrible enough for an adult to experience this type of heinous crime. One can only imagine what it does to a child who has been sexually violated. Living in a household with a monster called "Dad" would be excruciating. So it struck me especially hard when Diane shared with me her story of sexual abuse.

Wednesday, May 17, 1995

As I approached the first stop in the morning at the corner of Page and Jewett, the old school bus engine moaned like a constipated hippopotamus, trying to make the 6:36 a.m. pickup on time.

The first person to board that morning was Diane. She was a dark-haired, petite senior, attractive, and with eyes that shimmered like ocean pearls. Throughout the school year, Diane and her best friend Denise were always cordial and engaged in daily general conversation with me after boarding, which was welcomed because some high school students are very aloof, known for not being the most cordial group at times. But not Diane and Denise; they always returned morning and afternoon greetings prior to taking their seats.

After Diane took her seat that Wednesday morning, our conversation went as follows:

"Melvin, I won't be riding the bus on Friday."

"Thanks for telling me. I hope you have a nice day off from school."

"I won't, because I'm going to court."

"Sorry to hear that, Diane. I hope everything is okay!"

Diane then went on to tell me one of the most heart-gripping stories I have ever heard. She, along with her sister and little brother, were sexually molested by their father. Her court appearance on Friday was the first step in getting him put away from society. It was her younger sister that decided to break the code of silence; Diane's appearance was to confirm the years of abuse.

Remarkable as this may sound, it was not the perverted abuse suffered at the hands of their father that brought the siblings together—it was out of fear and concern that their new stepbrother and stepsister would also become victims of the monster who mentally and physically haunted them. Their father had remarried, with kids, courtesy of his second wife, at his disposal. Diane and her sister couldn't bear the fact that someone else would receive the same torture they endured.

I don't know why Diane decided to share this family tragedy with me. Maybe it just boils down to trust—trust that only a friend or bus driver could understand.

We must continue to denounce sexual abuse of children. This type of ignominious crime destroys lives

THE UNSPEAKABLE CRIME

at an unprecedented level, because kids are still timorous about reporting it. The first time should be the last for a monster that commits this type of unspeakable crime.

XII

The Last Day of School

June 16, 1995

Hot, hot, really hot and humid. That's how the day started out, with temperatures hovering in the mid-80s, along with matching Michigan humidity. It was finally here, the much-anticipated last day of school. Nothing, not even the heat that felt like a convection oven inside my old tin can school bus, could dampen the day. The last day of school was a half day session, with Thurston Elementary's dismissal time scheduled for 11:45 a.m.

I was counting down the hours like Dick Clark counting down another New Year's Eve in Times Square. The day before, I had said goodbye to my Bach afternoon kindergarten students. They were a great bunch of kids and I will miss them. Special thanks go out to Maia and Matthew's parents for the end of the school year gift they gave me. Thanks again for making my job so satisfying.

The majority of school bus drivers are very good at their stress-filled, demanding job. But you never really know what type of impact you have on your kids and parents until the last day of school. That last day of school brings unbridled displays of tear-filled emotions,

SCHOOL BUS DRIVER

along with the sense that you really made a difference in people's lives.

The full magnitude of that day came when Froggy walked up to me, stopped, looked up, and said, "Melvin, I'm really going to miss you," with tears in his eyes. Emotionally choked up, I reached down, hugged him like a long-lost relative and called his real name saying, "I'm really going to miss you, too!"

Thanks for riding with me.

Brock's Barbers: Thanks for all your support, Mr. Brock.

SCHOOL BUS DRIVER

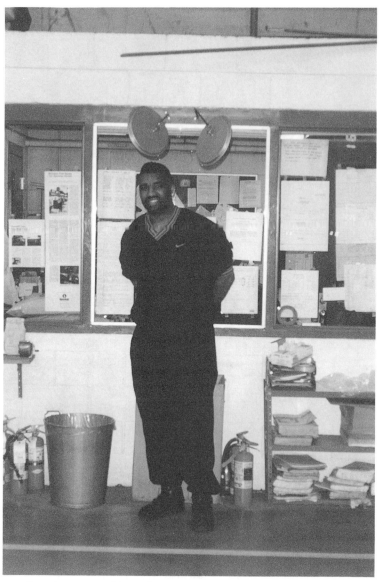

Brother Darrold Bridges, your unconditional devotion helped make this book possible.

Epilogue

I hope this book was effective in educating you about different aspects of transportation and education. There was a tremendous amount of adversity and hardship I had to overcome in completing this book. If it were not for my strong belief in God, family support, and devoted friends, this book could not have happened. The nay-sayers were numerous!

That always seems to be the case when you are working on accomplishing a goal. The one thing I always kept in my mind was the responsibility I owed the kids, parents, general public, and friends in bringing to light the tremendous job school bus drivers do, despite the everyday challenges the job presents. To all those kids and parents who made my job so fulfilling throughout the years, this book was for you.

> Melvin D. Latnie Jr.
> Transportation Team Leader
> Ann Arbor Public Schools

SCHOOL BUS DRIVER

Charles, Jessica, Felecia